Dear Parent:
Your child's love of reading

Every child learns to read in a different way and at his or her own speed. Some go back and forth between reading levels and read favorite books again and again. Others read through each level in order. You can help your young reader improve and become more confident by encouraging his or her own interests and abilities. From books your child reads with you to the first books he or she reads alone, there are I Can Read Books for every stage of reading:

SHARED READING
Basic language, word repetition, and whimsical illustrations, ideal for sharing with your emergent reader

BEGINNING READING
Short sentences, familiar words, and simple concepts for children eager to read on their own

READING WITH HELP
Engaging stories, longer sentences, and language play for developing readers

READING ALONE
Complex plots, challenging vocabulary, and high-interest topics for the independent reader

ADVANCED READING
Short paragraphs, chapters, and exciting themes for the perfect bridge to chapter books

I Can Read Books have introduced children to the joy of reading since 1957. Featuring award-winning authors and illustrators and a fabulous cast of beloved characters, I Can Read Books set the standard for beginning readers.

A lifetime of discovery begins with the magical words "I Can Read!"

Visit www.icanread.com for information
on enriching your child's reading experience.

I Can Read Book® is a trademark of HarperCollins Publishers.

Guinness World Records: Fun with Food
© 2016 Guinness World Records Limited.
The words GUINNESS WORLD RECORDS and related logos are trademarks of Guinness World Records Limited.
All records and information accurate as of August 1, 2015.

For information address HarperCollins Children's Books, a division of HarperCollins Publishers, 195 Broadway, New York, NY 10007.
www.icanread.com

Library of Congress Control Number: 2015947489
ISBN 978-0-06-234189-1 (trade bdg.) — ISBN 978-0-06-234188-4 (pbk.)
Typography by Erica De Chavez

16 17 18 19 20 SCP 10 9 8 7 6 5 4 3 2 1   ❖   First Edition

I Can Read!

READING 2 WITH HELP

GUINNESS WORLD RECORDS

FUN WITH FOOD

by Christy Webster

HARPER
An Imprint of HarperCollinsPublishers

People do *eggs*-traordinary things with their food!

Corey Perras from Canada set the record for **most eggs cracked in 1 hour using one hand—** 3,031.

Do you like a big breakfast? In South Africa, Kellogg's made the **largest bowl of cereal**. It held 572 pounds of cornflakes!

Mike Cuzzacrea from New York took his breakfast on the road. He ran the **fastest marathon while flipping a pancake**. It took him 3 hours, 2 minutes, and 27 seconds to finish the race.

Martina Servaty from Germany used her feet in a different way. She squeezed the **most grape juice in 2 minutes with her feet**—5.36 gallons.

A good cup of coffee in the morning can take Martin Bacon far—fast! Martin, from the United Kingdom, built the **fastest coffee-powered car**. It goes more than 65 miles per hour!

In 2012, a total of 1,400 people got hands-on with salad at the same time in Singapore. That's the **most people tossing salad**!

A communications company in the Netherlands called DENK made the **largest bowl of soup**. It was 7,042 gallons. That's a big lunch!

A big grilled-cheese sandwich
would taste good with that soup.
The Cabot Creamery of Vermont made
the world's **largest grilled sandwich**.
It weighed 320 pounds!

There is no such thing
as a free lunch. . . .
The **most expensive hot dog**
cost $169 in Seattle, Washington.
It had fancy toppings,
like caviar and truffles!

The **most expensive hamburger**, meanwhile, cost $5,000 in Oregon! Don't forget to order in advance, though. It takes two days to prepare!

A movie theater in Croatia
made the **largest box of popcorn**.
It was 1,857 cubic feet.
A big snack for the big screen!

52,73m³
51,51m³
50,03m³

47,91m³

45,57m³

The **oldest candy shop** in the world has been open since 1827. Its name, appropriately, is The Oldest Sweet Shop in England.

A peanut butter and jelly sandwich is a great snack.

Patrick Bertoletti from Illinois ate the **most peanut butter and jelly sandwiches in 1 minute—6!**

Takeru Kobayashi from Japan

is a competitive eater.

He can eat food a lot faster

than most people.

In 2009, he achieved the **most**

hot dogs eaten in 3 minutes—6!

Tafzi Ahmed from Germany head-butted 43 watermelons into pieces.

That's the **most watermelons smashed with the head in 1 minute!**

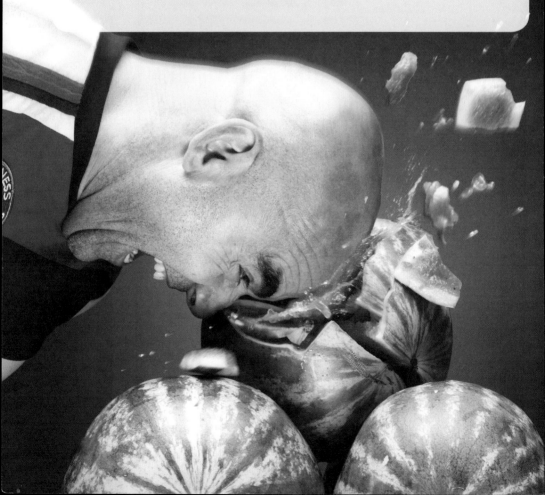

It's pizza time!

Tony Gemignani from Minnesota
spun the **largest pizza base
in 2 minutes**.
It was 33.2 inches wide!

Antonio Ramos García
brought 162 people together
for a record-breaking
meat-and-greet in Spain:
the **most people slicing meat**!

A meat dinner

calls for mashed potatoes!

Joël Robuchon and

the French theme park Futuroscope

made the **largest serving**

of mashed potatoes.

It was 2,297 pounds.

The **largest serving of macaroni and cheese** was made in New Orleans by two cooking companies. It weighed 2,469 pounds.

A dinner needs vegetables, too. Scott and Mardie Robb presented the **heaviest turnip** at the Alaska State Fair in 2004. It weighed 39 pounds, 3 ounces.

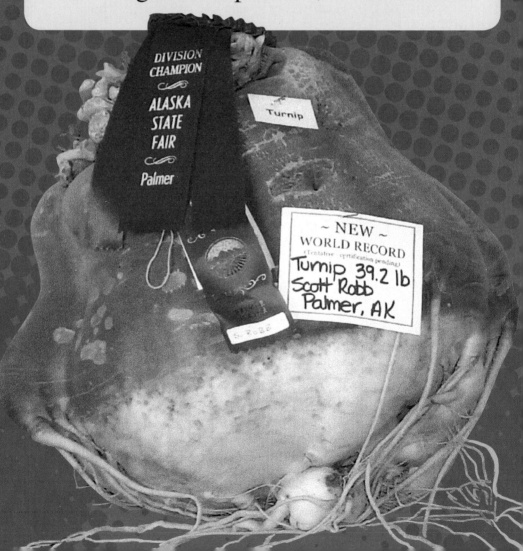

A cooking school in Indonesia
made a special dessert in 2008.
Standing over 108 feet high,
it is the **tallest cake** ever.

Edith Fuchs from Indiana
never runs out of places
to keep cookies.
That's because she has the **largest
collection of cookie jars**!
She has 2,653 of them.

Jerry Mumma spent $3,100 on a peanut butter and banana pie! It was the **most expensive pie sold at an auction**. It was baked by Jarra Mumma, his granddaughter, in Missouri.

Sometimes after dinner people eat cheese for dessert. In Canada, the **largest cheese made from cow's milk** was a cheddar. It weighed over 28 tons. A special truck had to carry it.

A team of 12 people
in the United Kingdom
made the **most cups of tea
in 1 hour**.
They poured out 1,608 cups!

After all that food,

you may want a hot drink.

But the **largest cup of coffee**

would keep you awake for weeks!

Brewed by Caffé Bene of South Korea,

this cup of joe is 3,758.7 gallons.

The record for the **most canned drinks opened by a parrot** was set by Zac the Macaw from San Jose.
He opened 35 fizzy drinks in 1 minute using just his beak!

Akiko Obata from Japan
has the **largest collection
of food-related items**.
It includes 8,083 objects—
everything from food magnets
to food key chains.
She must love amazing eats, too!